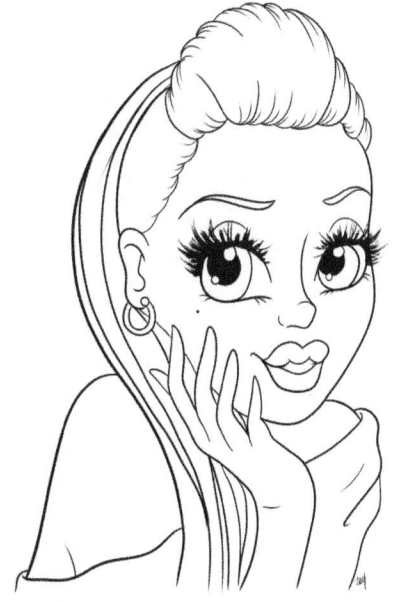

Illustrations by T

It's just a Flirt!

A FLIRTY COLORING BOOK FOR ADULTS. ADD SOME PZAZZ!

Illustrated by Tamara van Wijk

~ When life throws you lemons...
draw on them ~

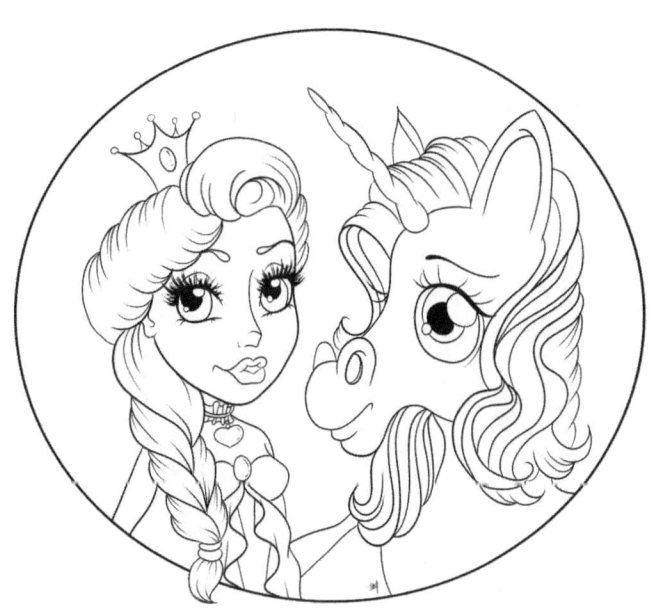

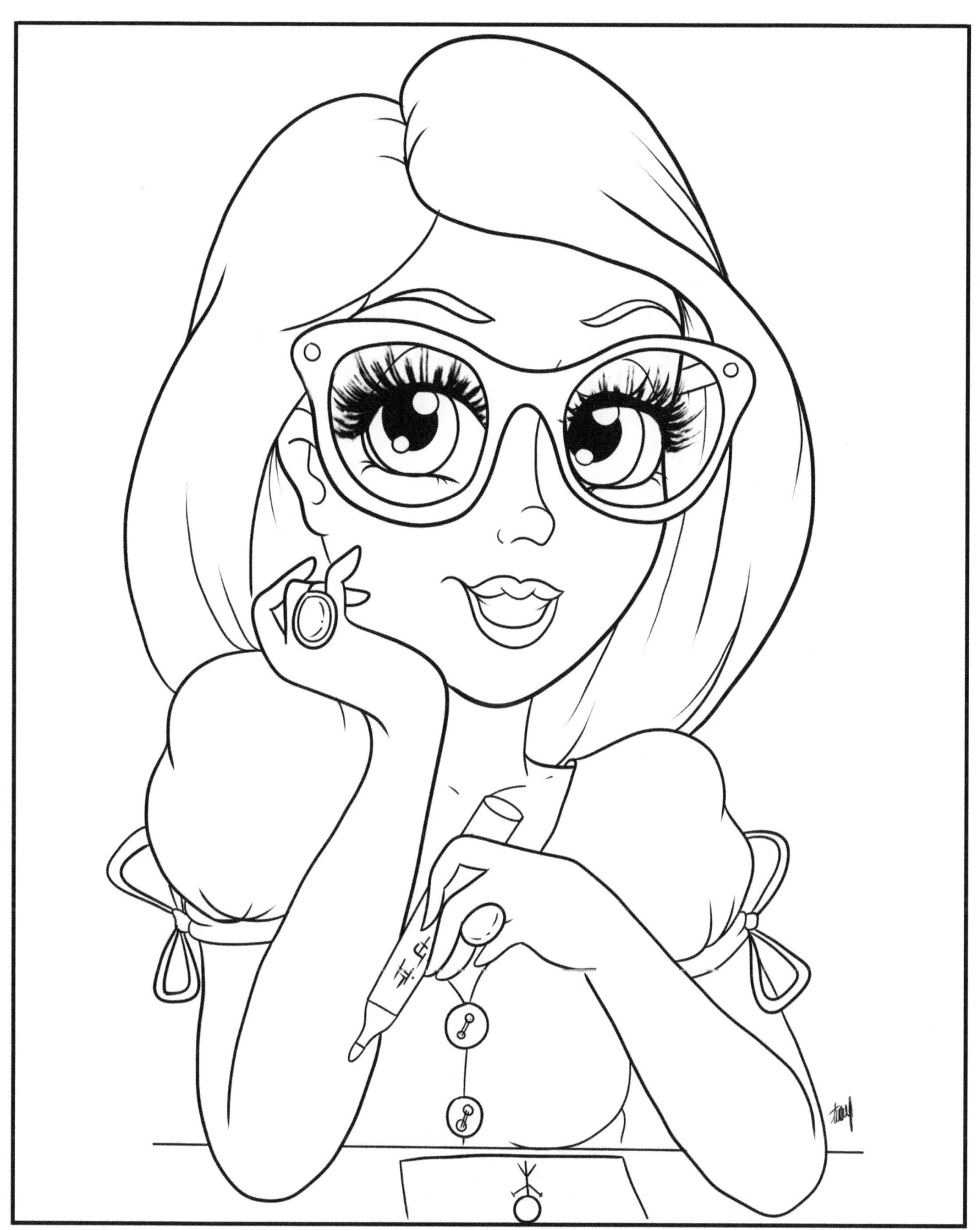

Illustrations by T.

Tamara van Wijk

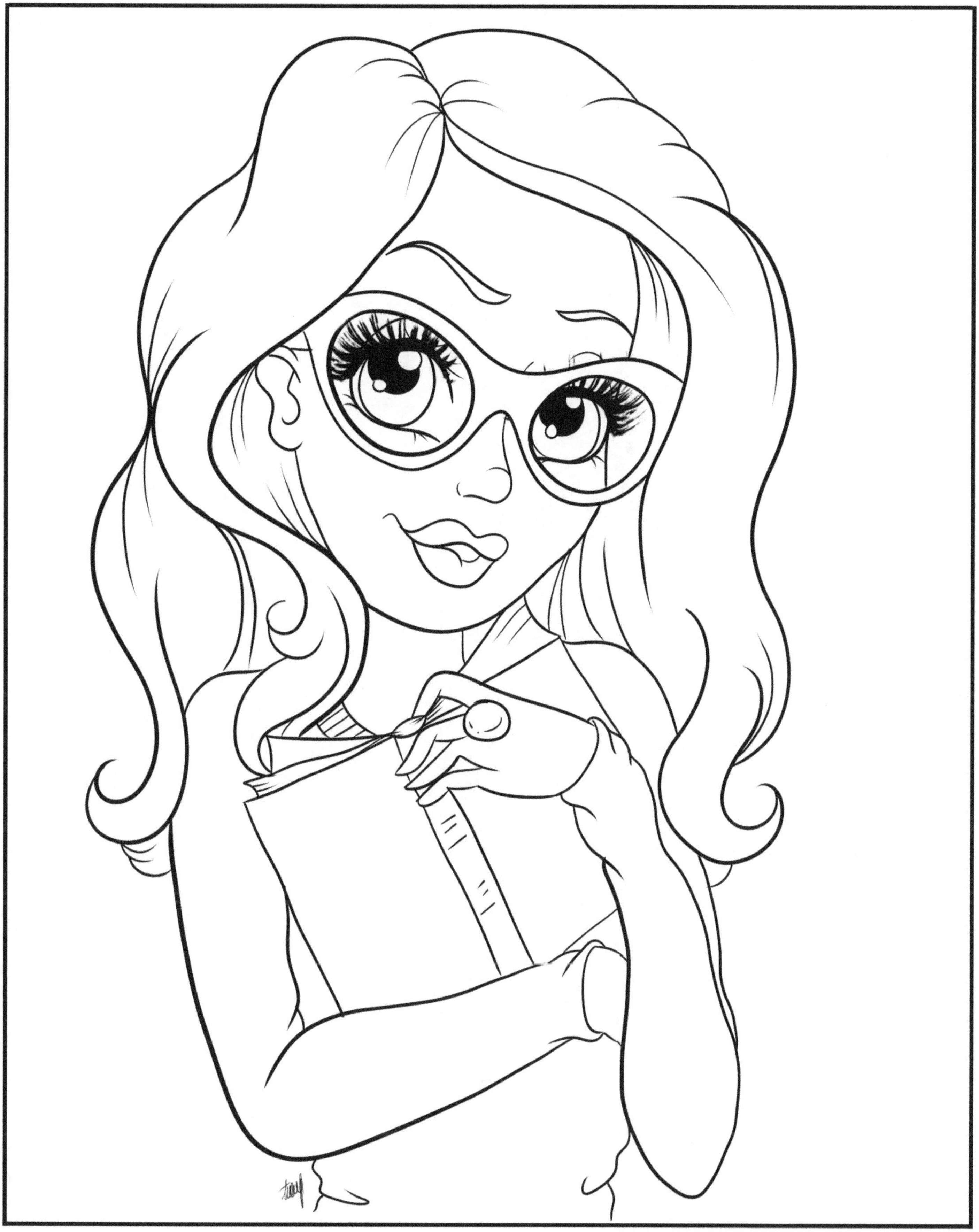

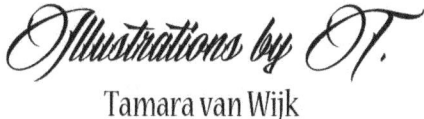

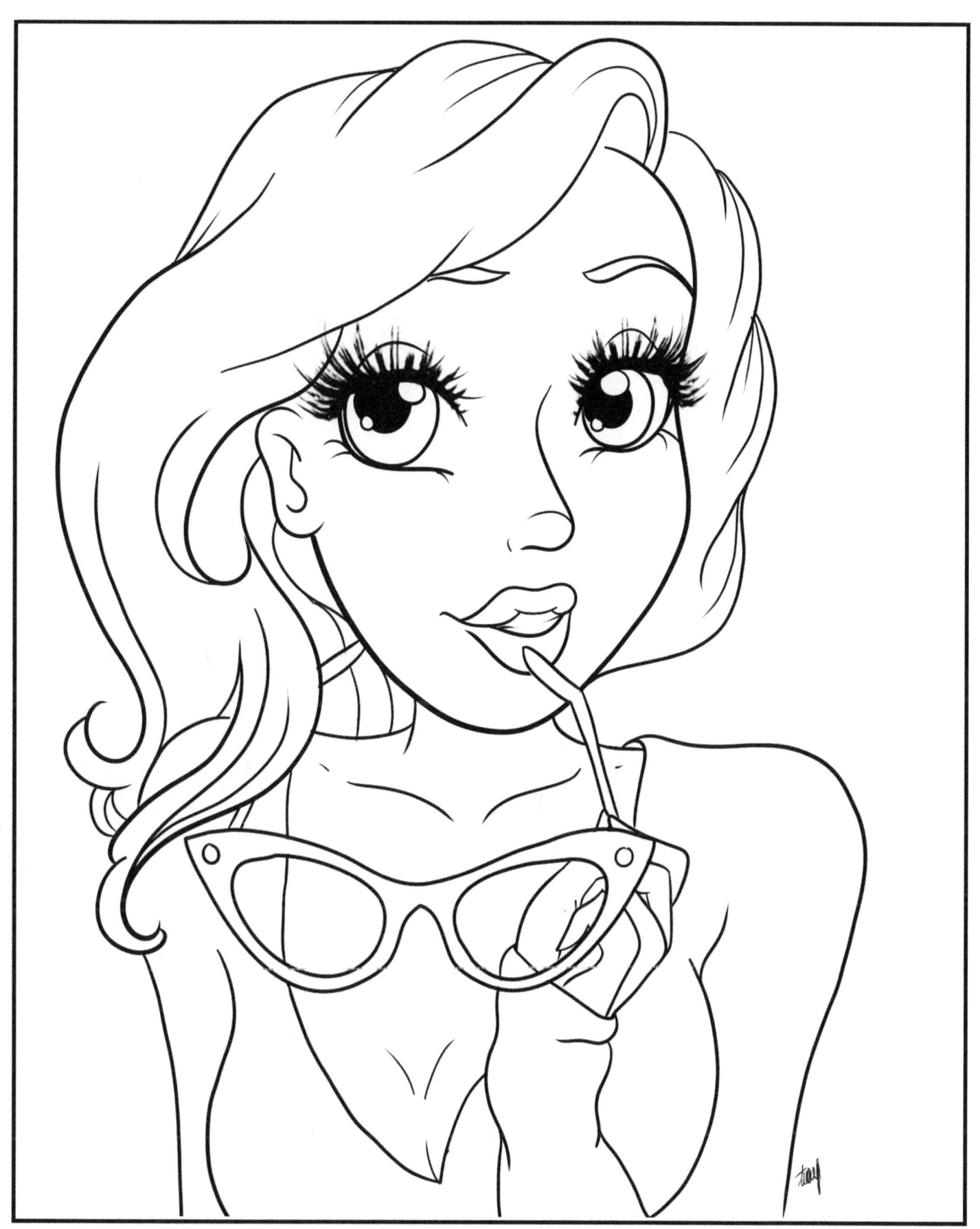

Illustrations by T.

Tamara van Wijk

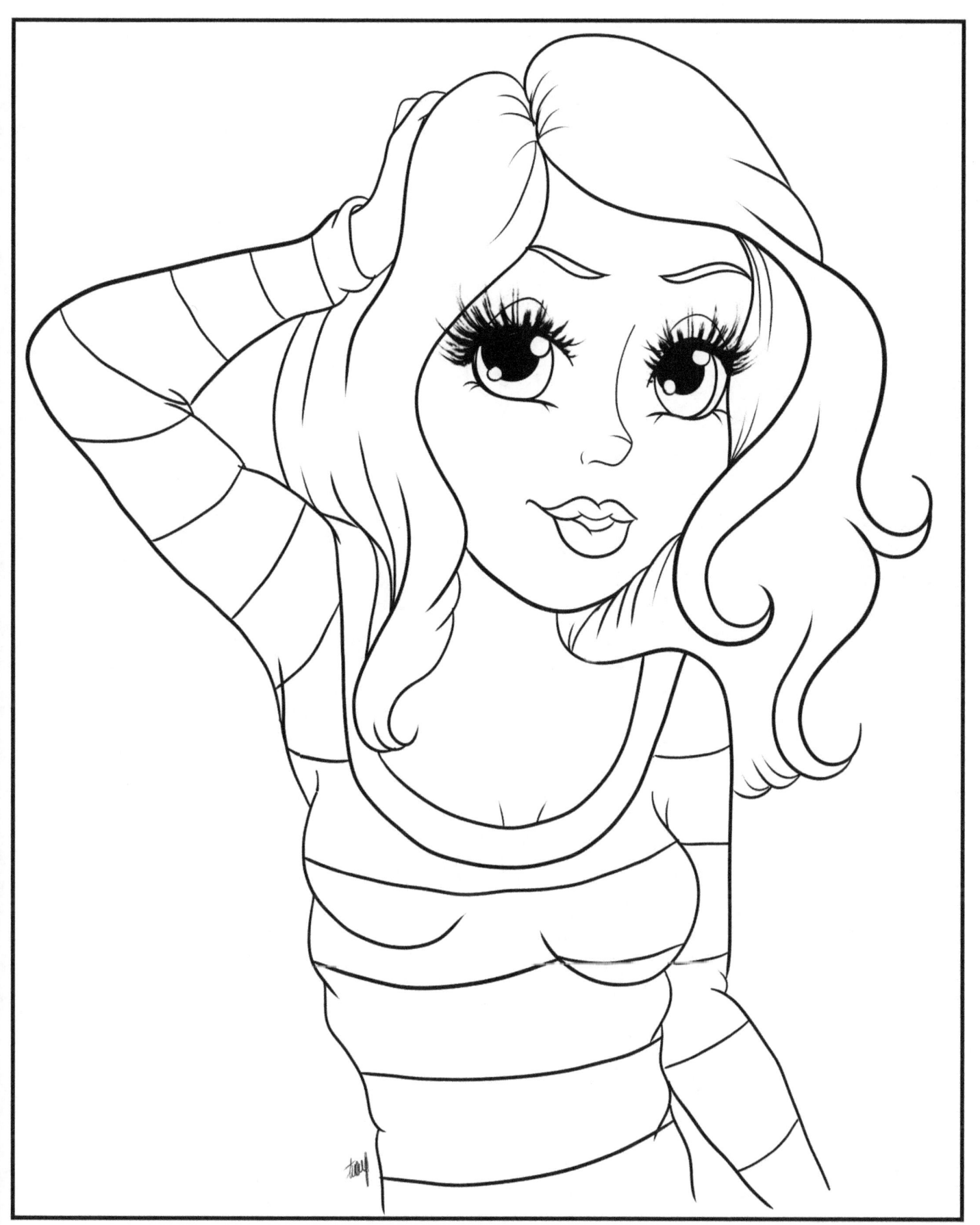

Illustrations by T.
Tamara van Wijk

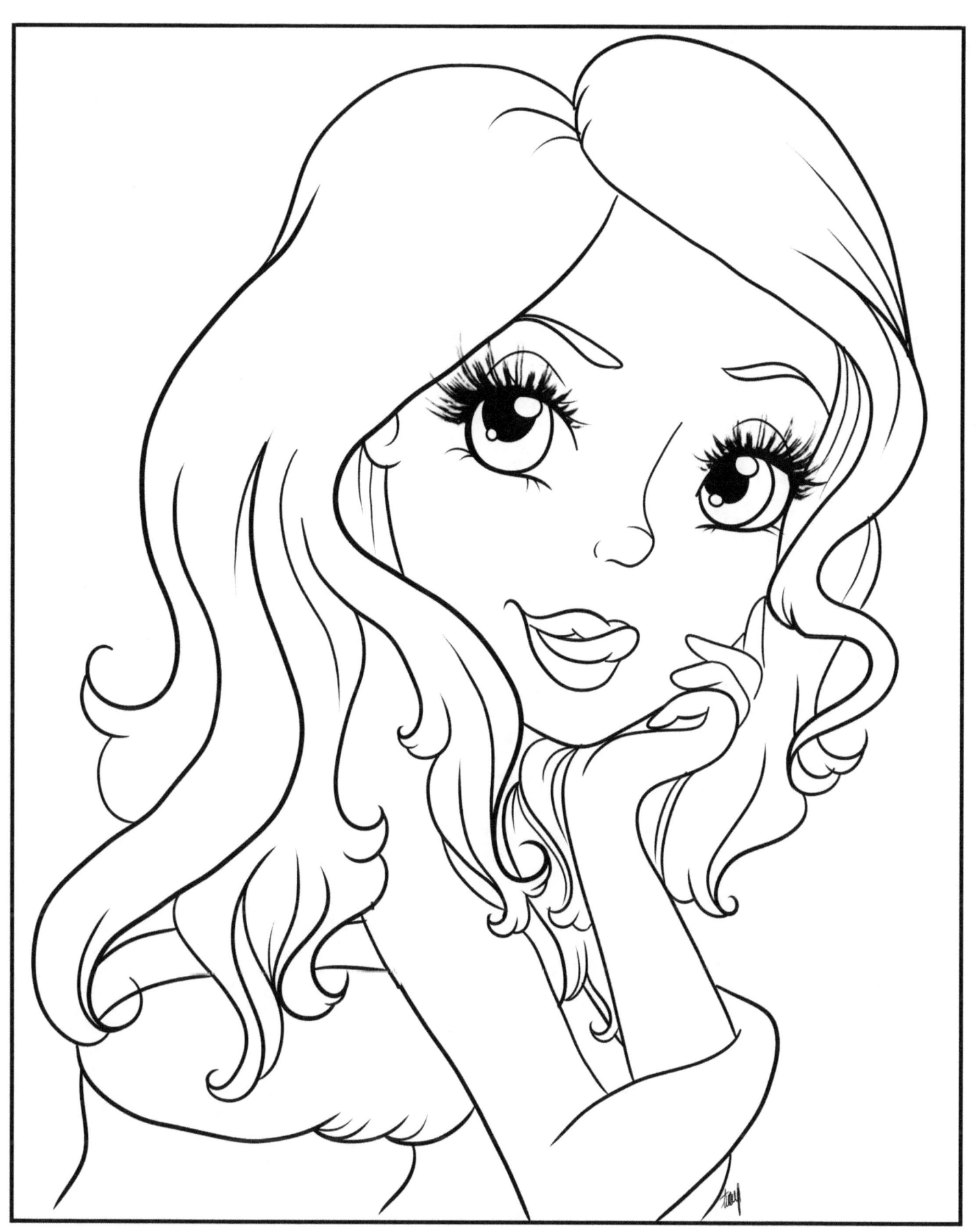

Illustrations by T.

Tamara van Wijk

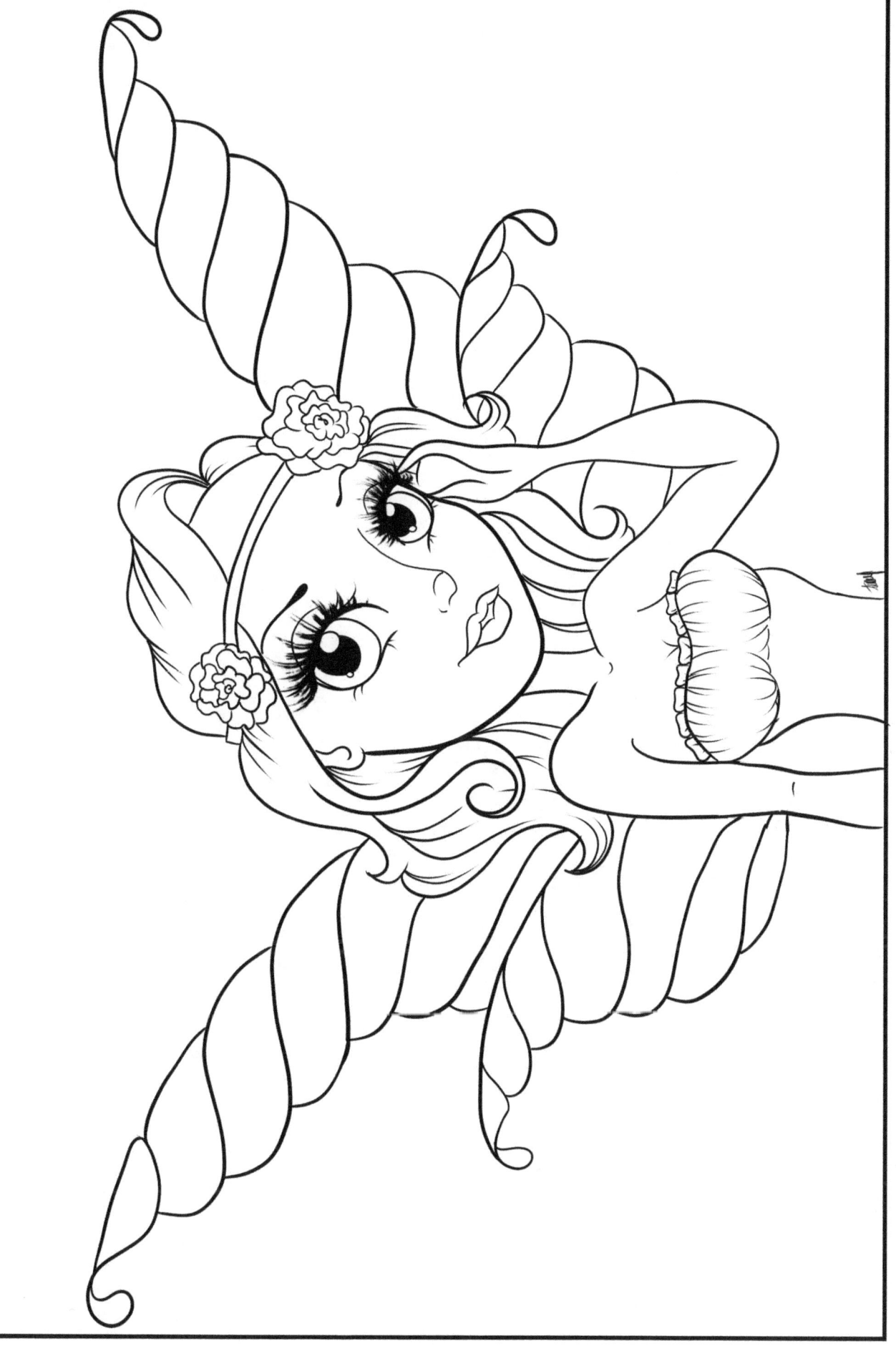

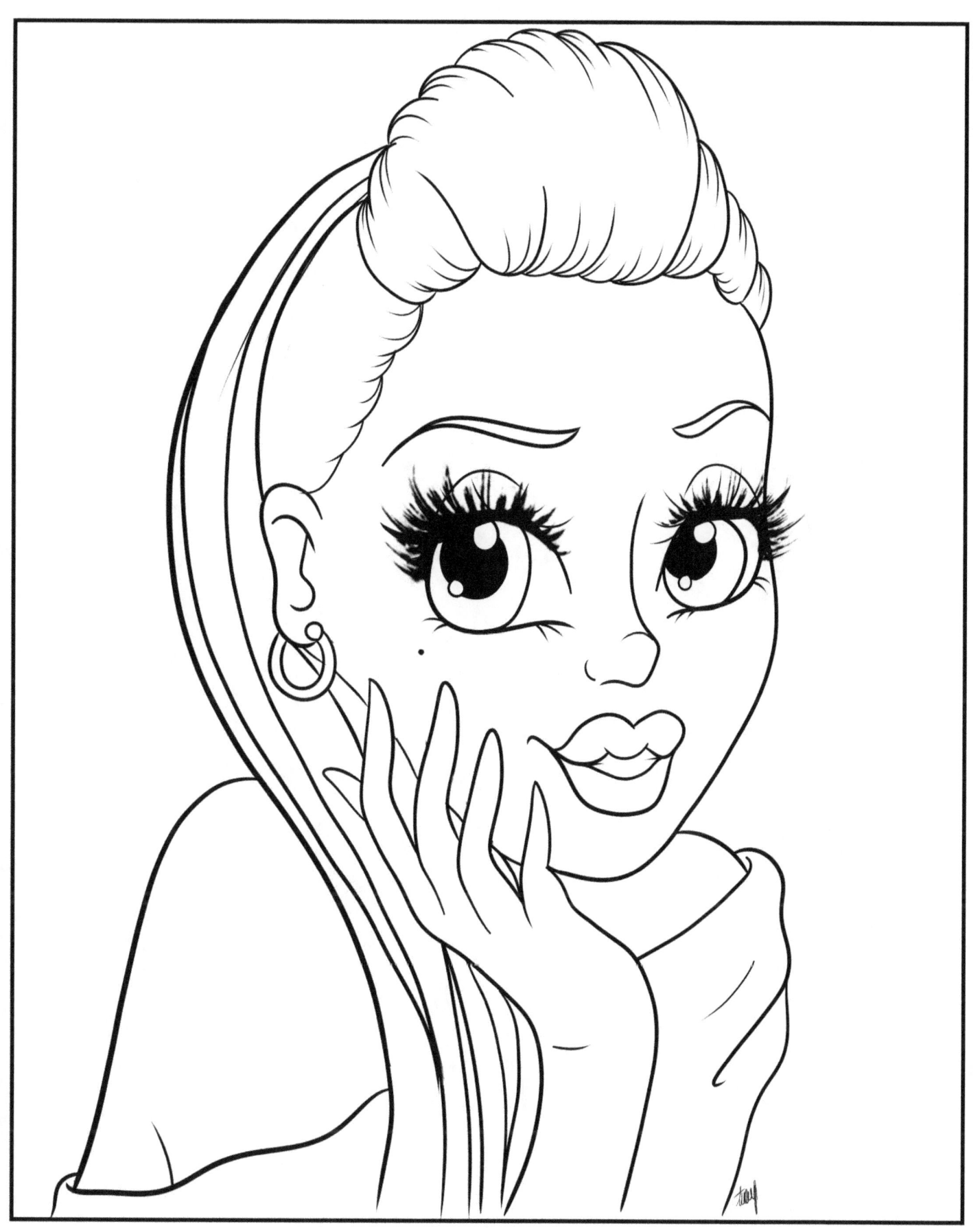

Illustrations by T.

Tamara van Wijk

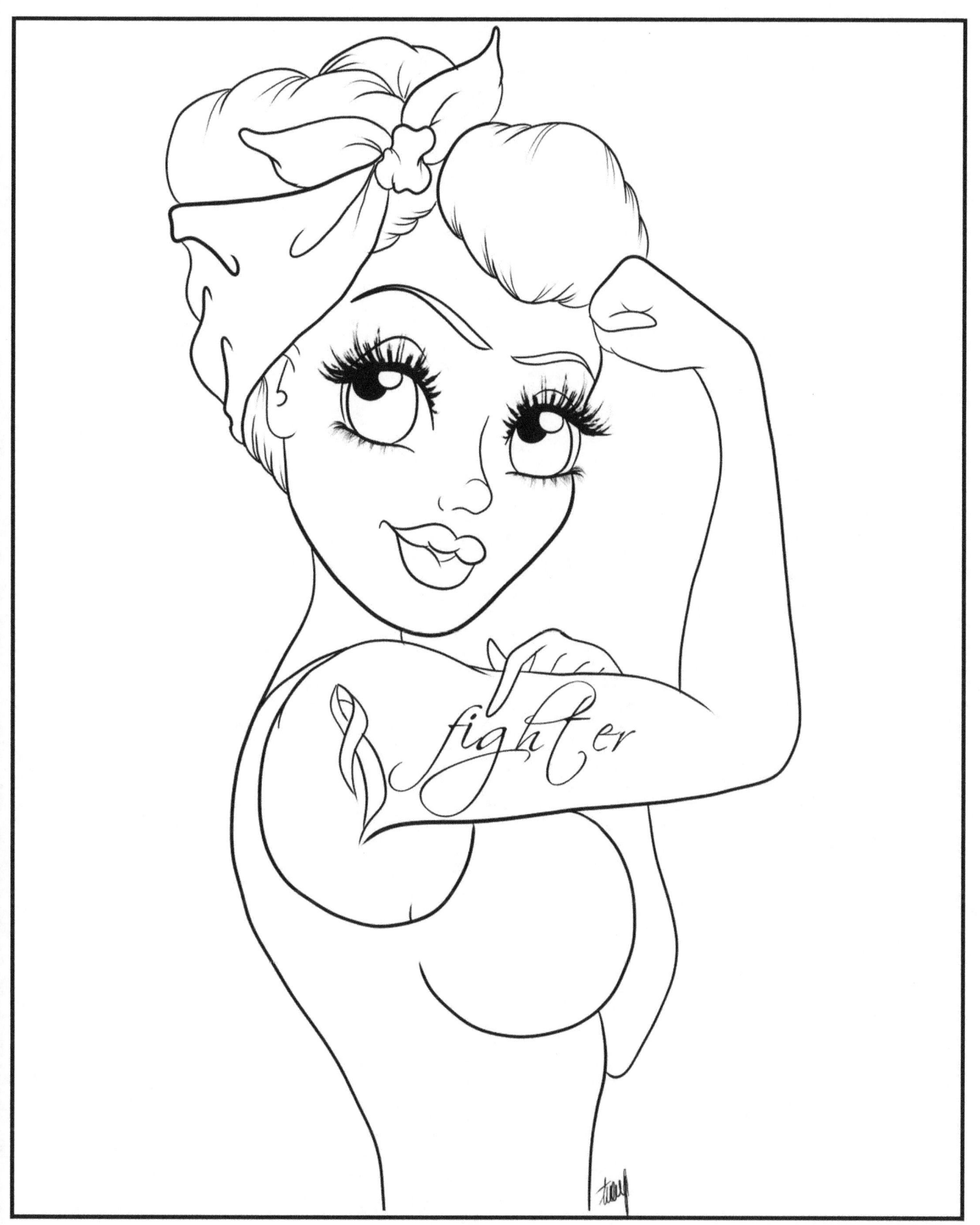

The word "fighter" appears as a tattoo on the figure's arm.

Illustrations by T.

Tamara van Wijk

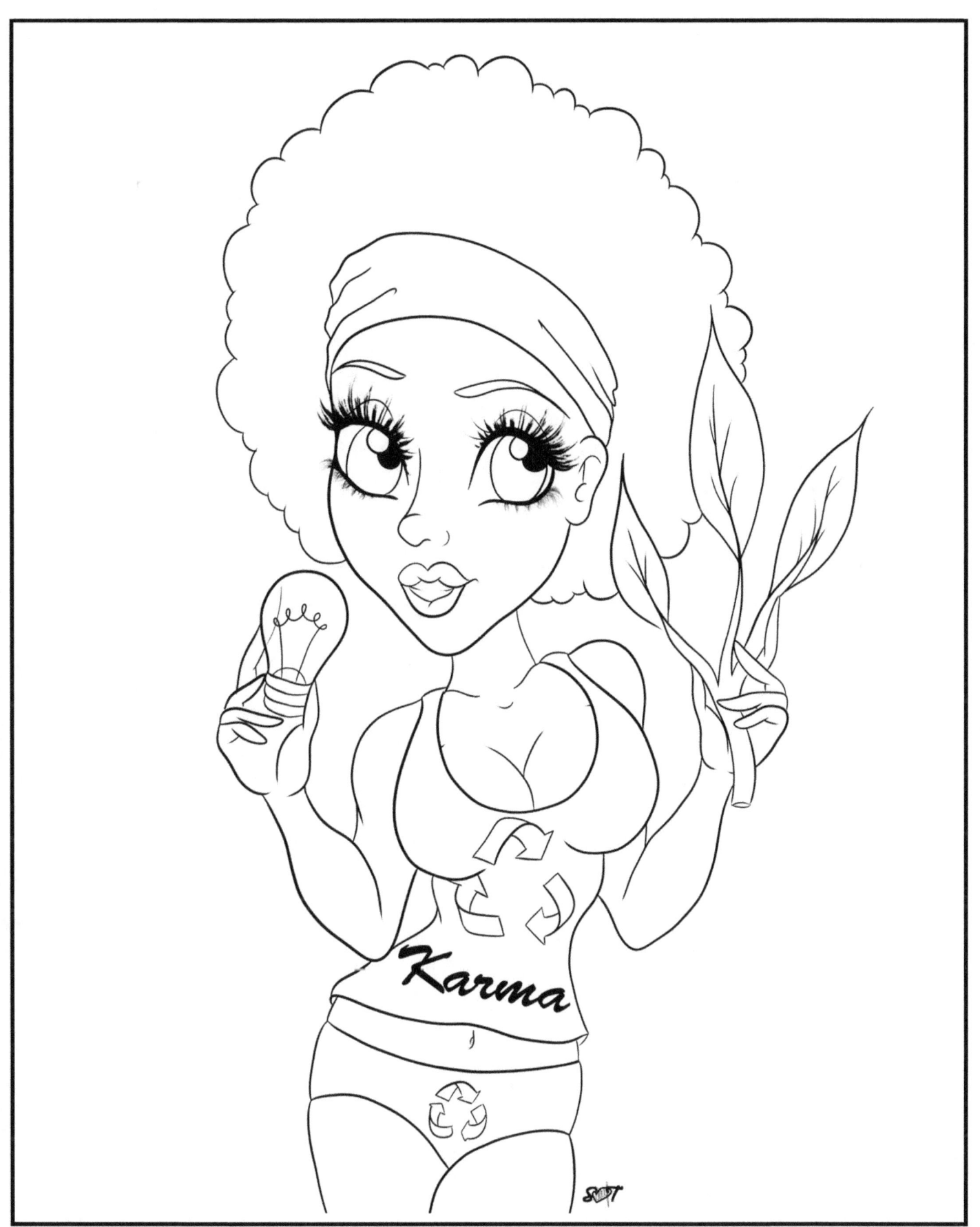

Illustrations by T.

Tamara van Wijk

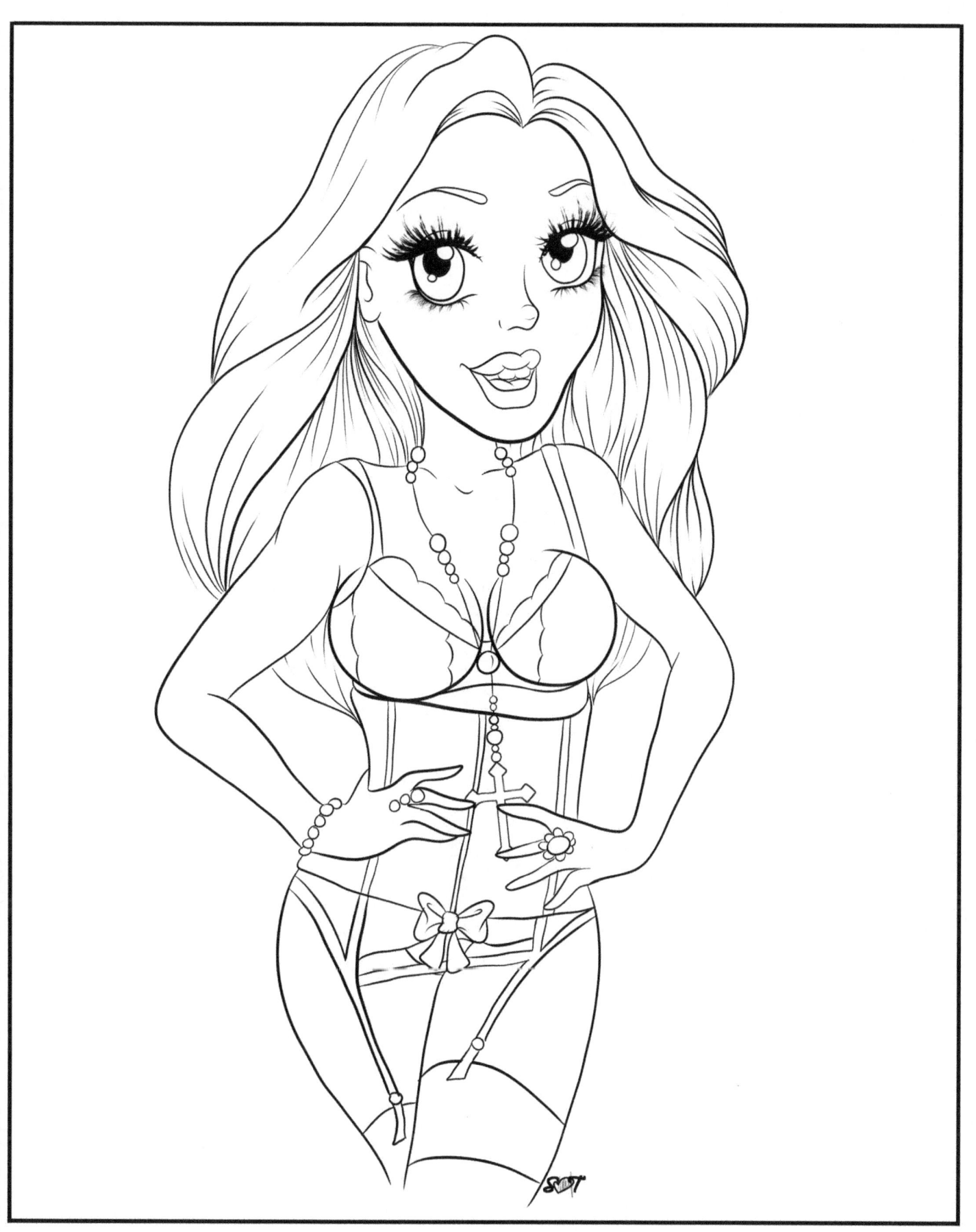

Illustrations by T.

Tamara van Wijk

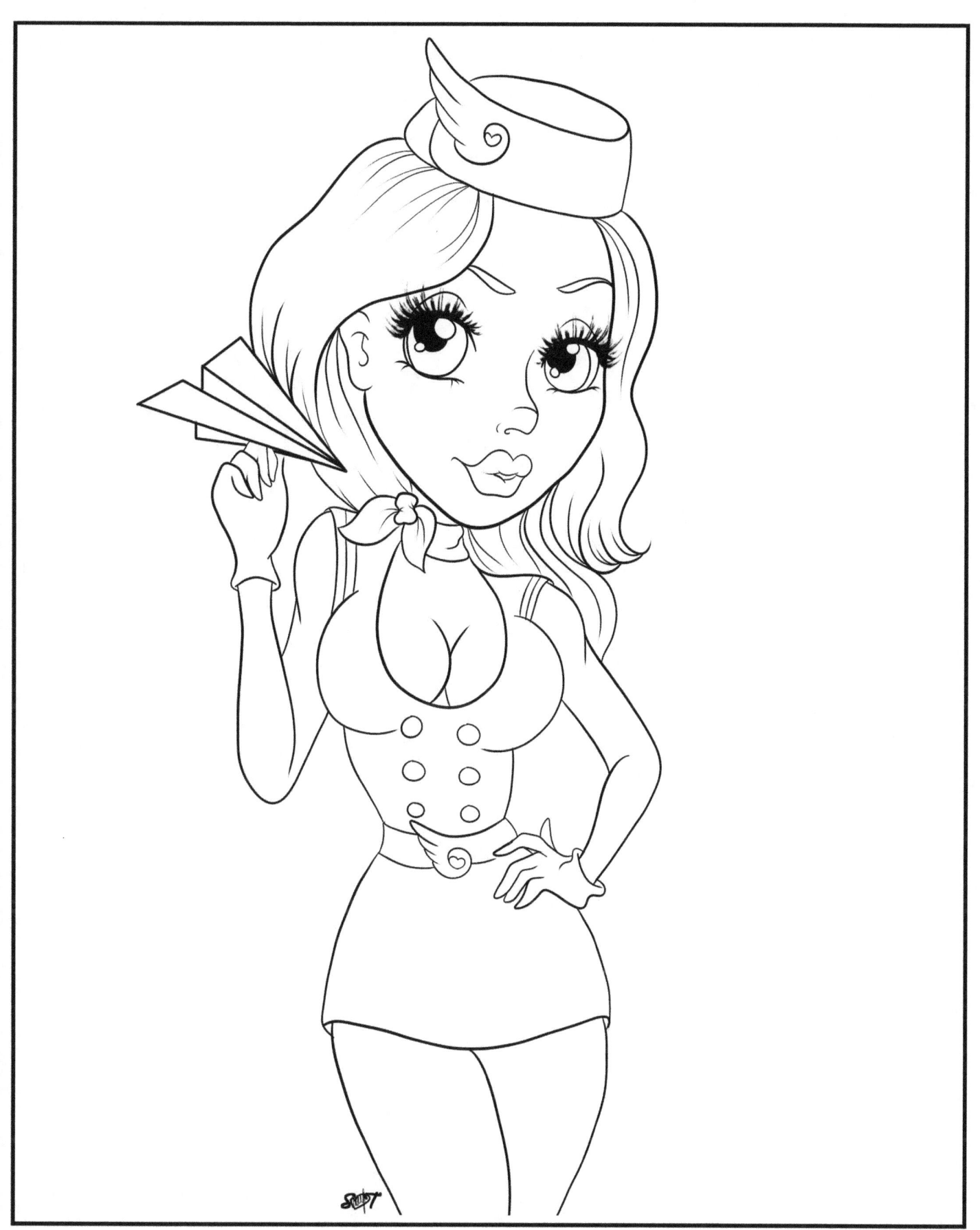

Illustrations by T.

Tamara van Wijk

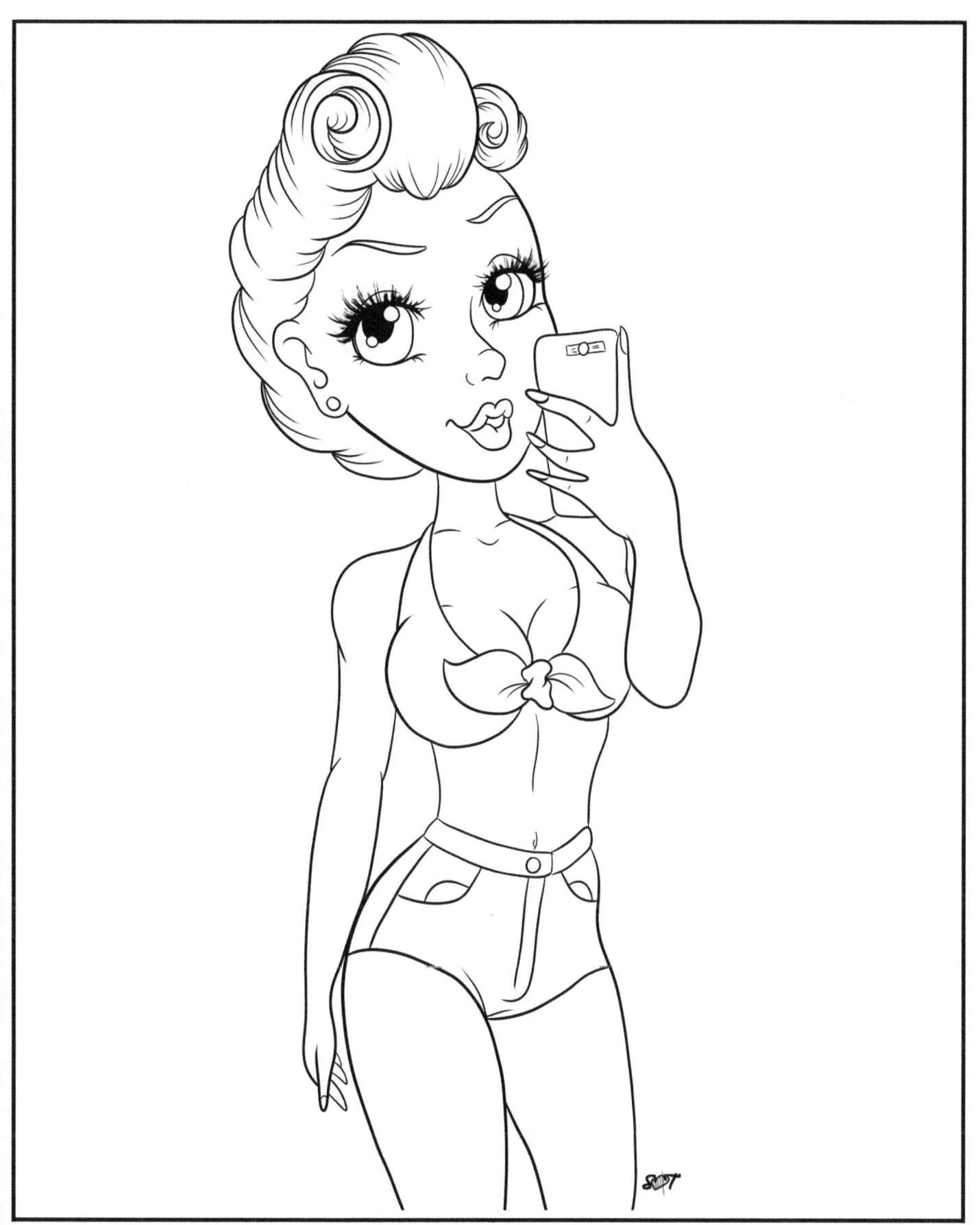

Illustrations by O.T.

Tamara van Wijk

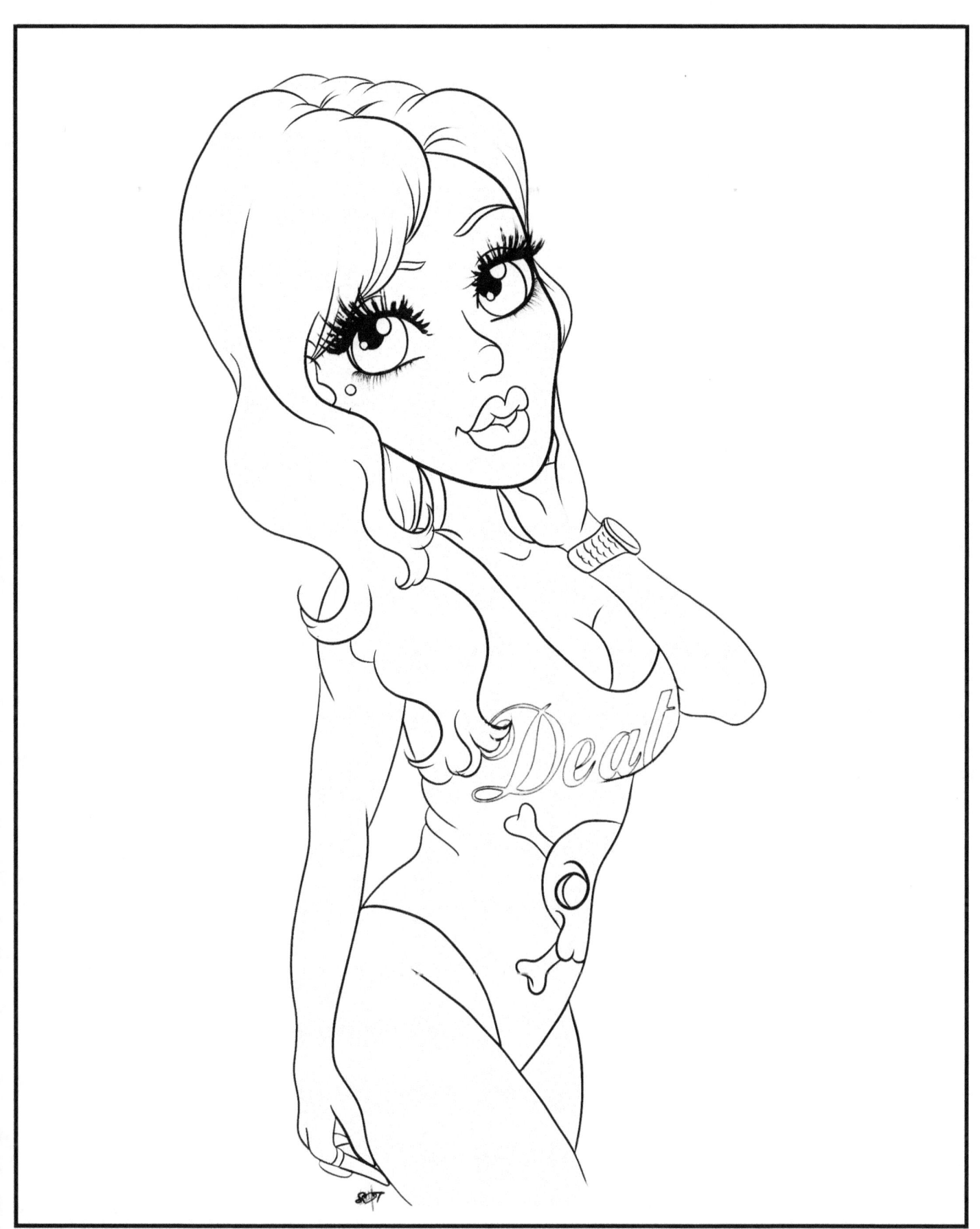

Illustrations by T.

Tamara van Wijk

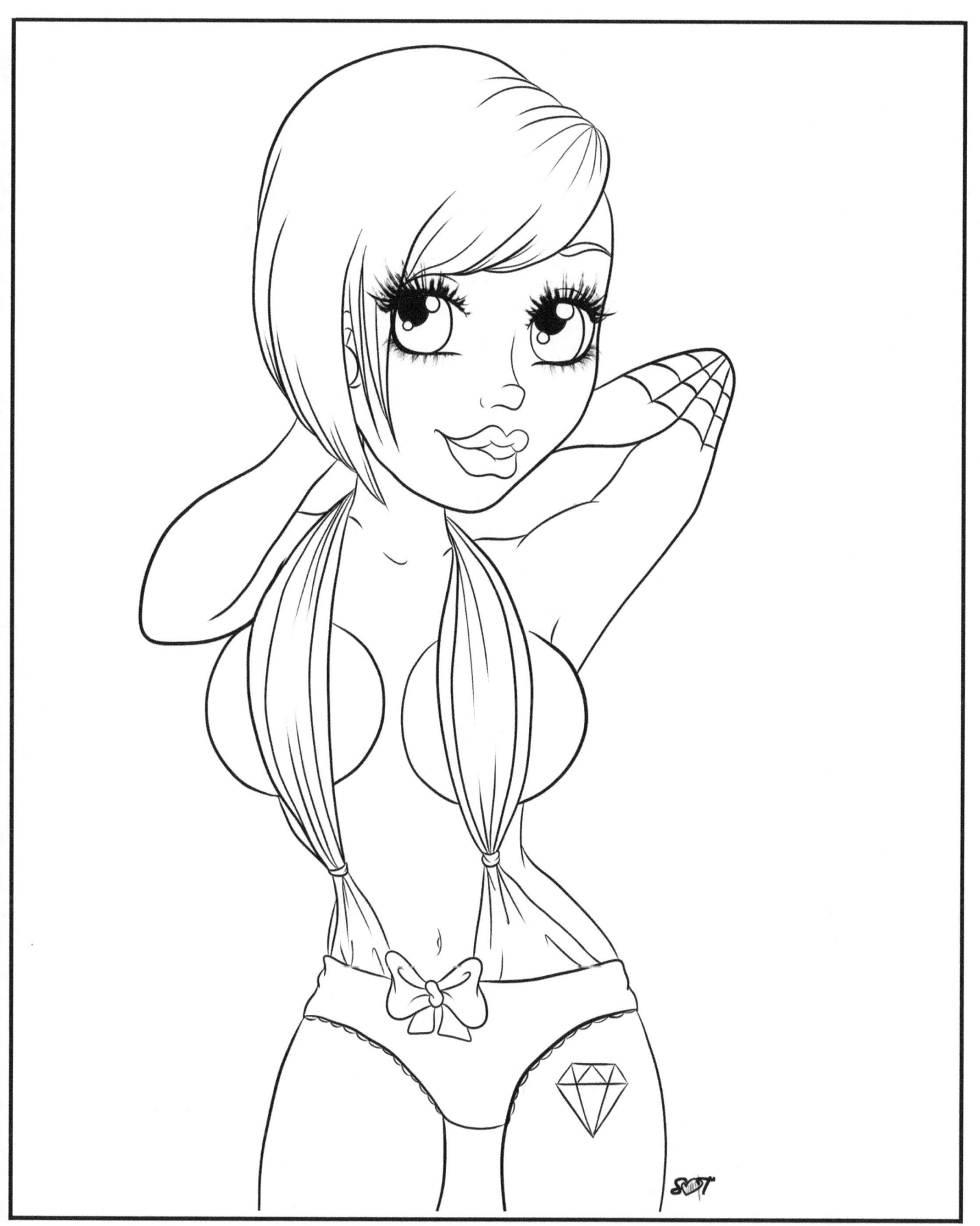

Illustrations by T.

Tamara van Wijk

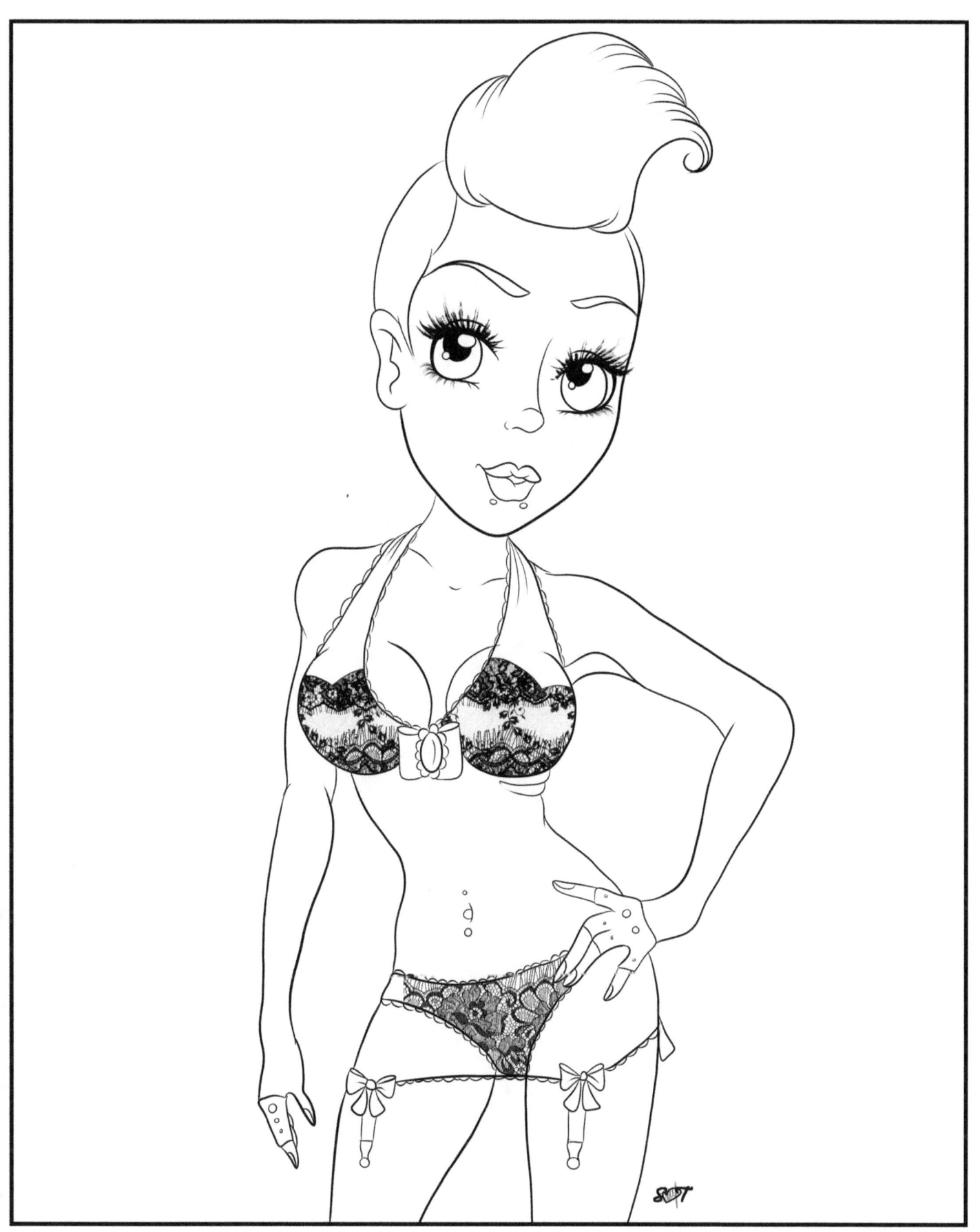

Illustrations by T.

Tamara van Wijk

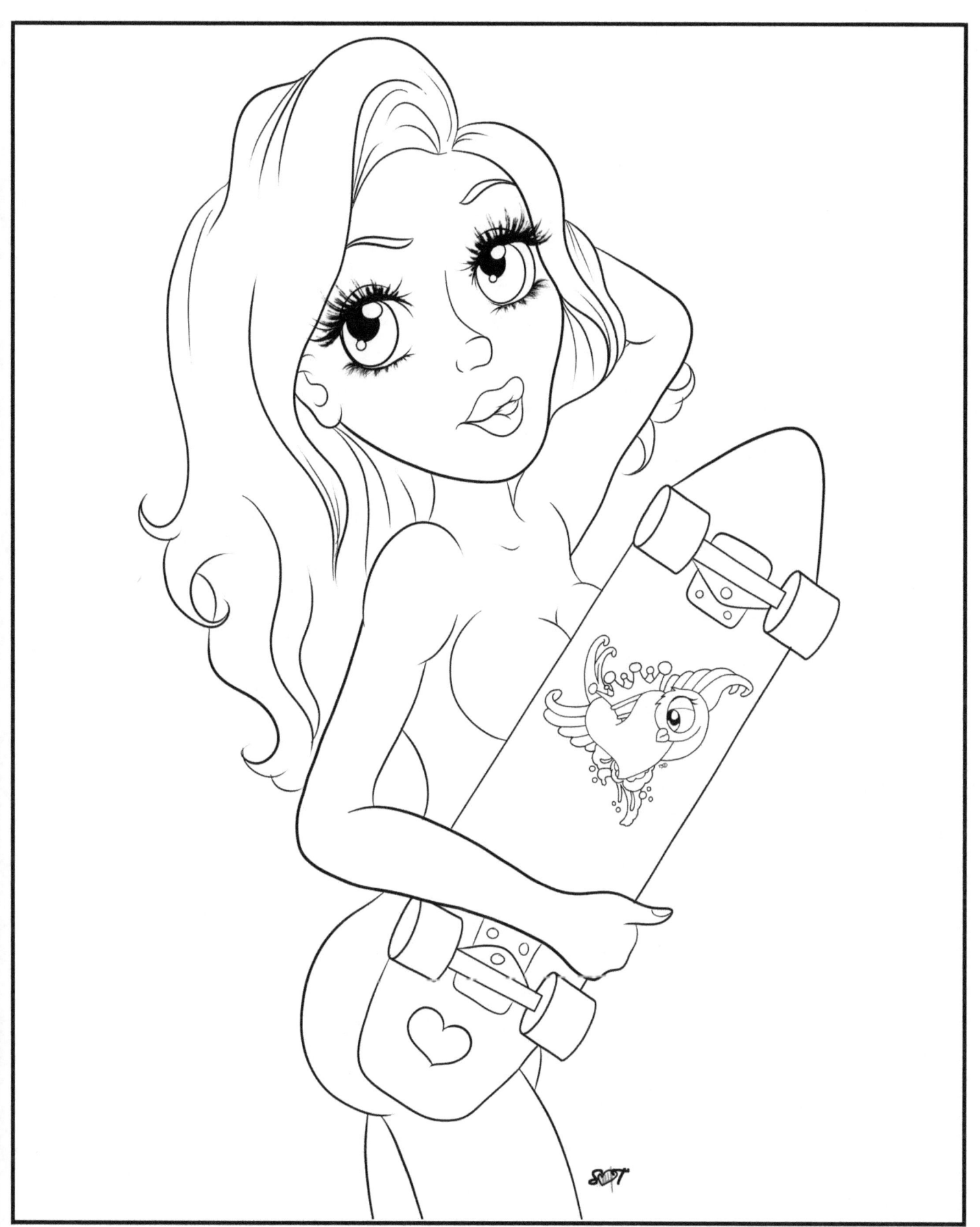

Illustrations by T.

Tamara van Wijk

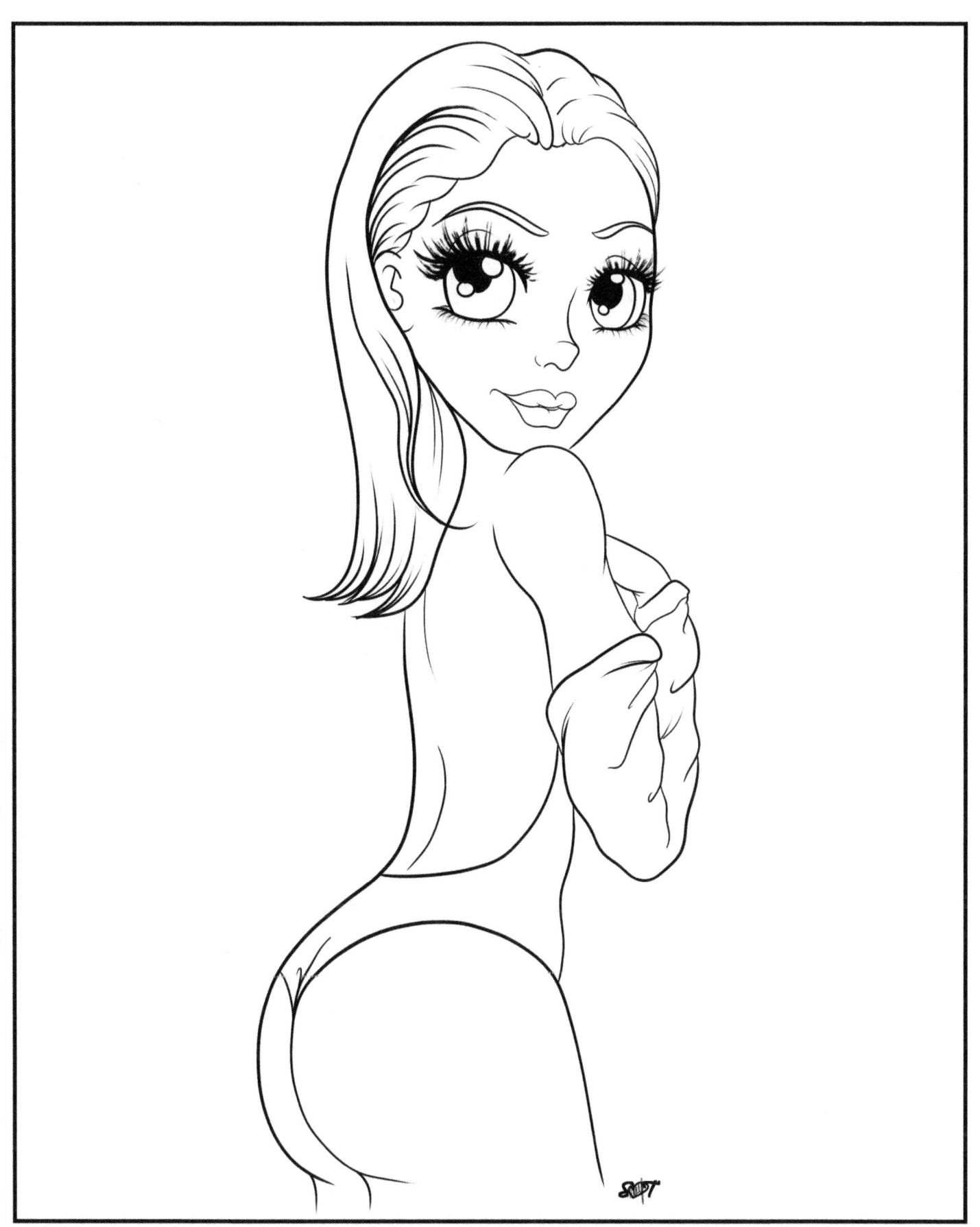

Illustrations by T.

Tamara van Wijk

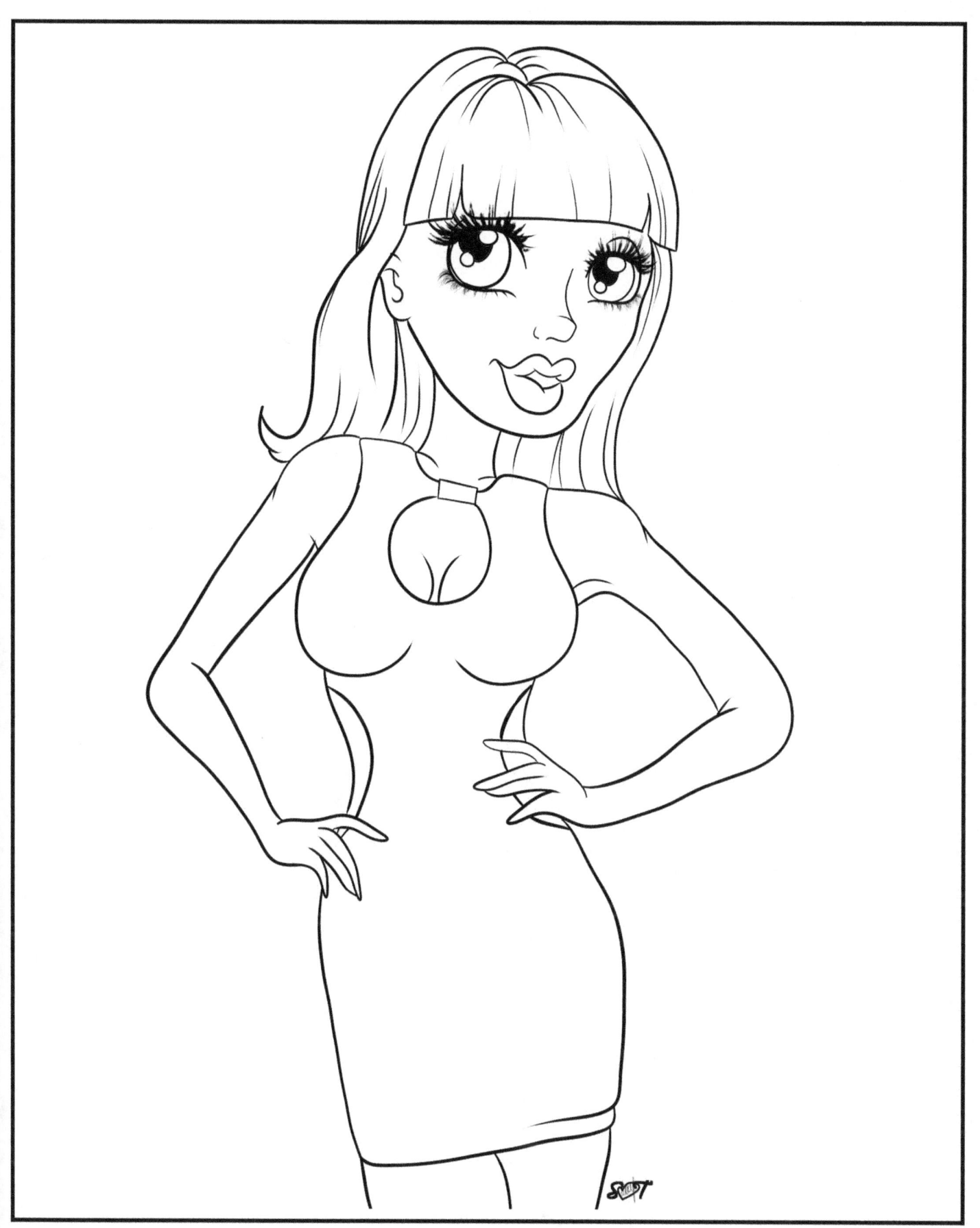

Illustrations by T.

Tamara van Wijk

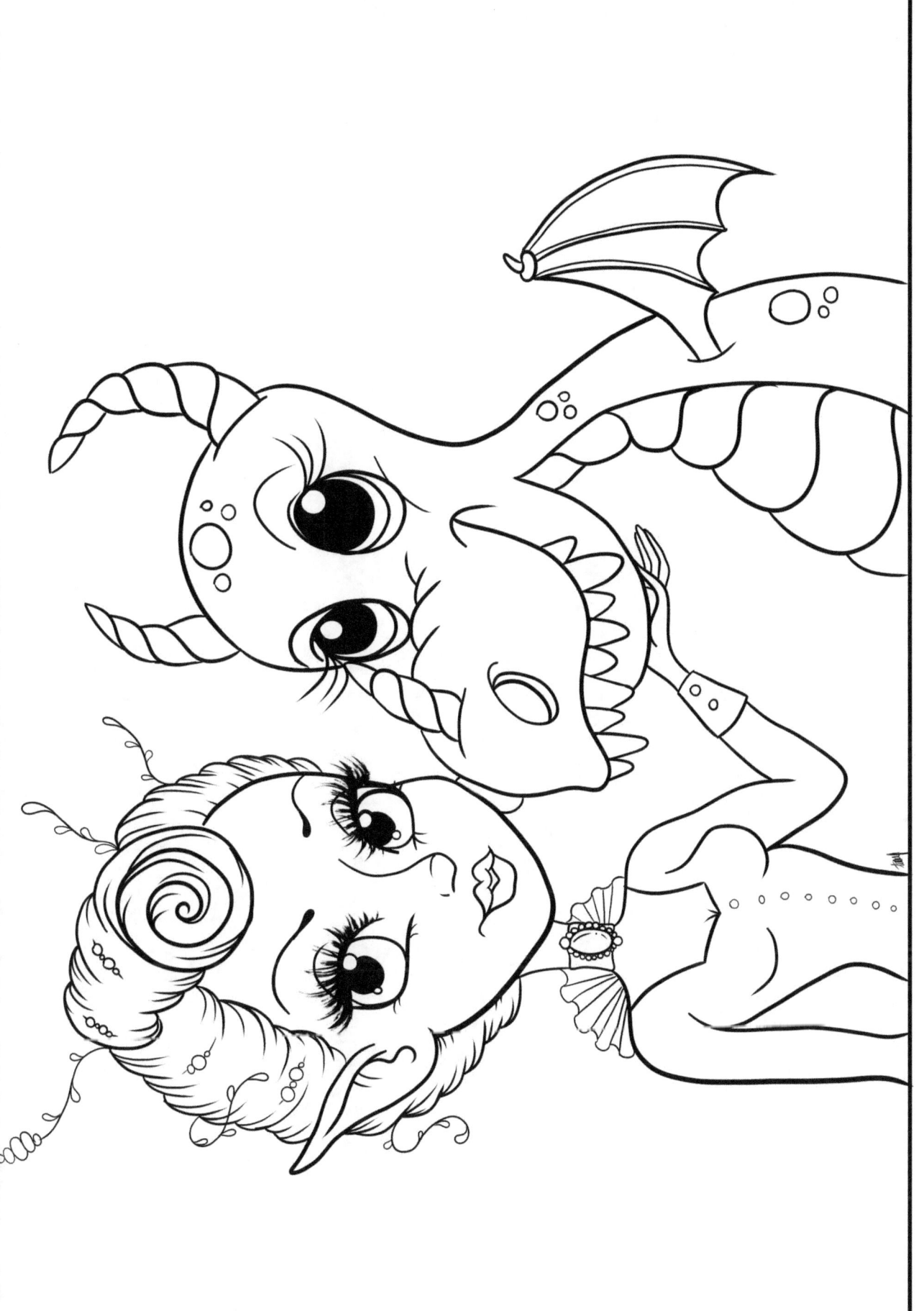

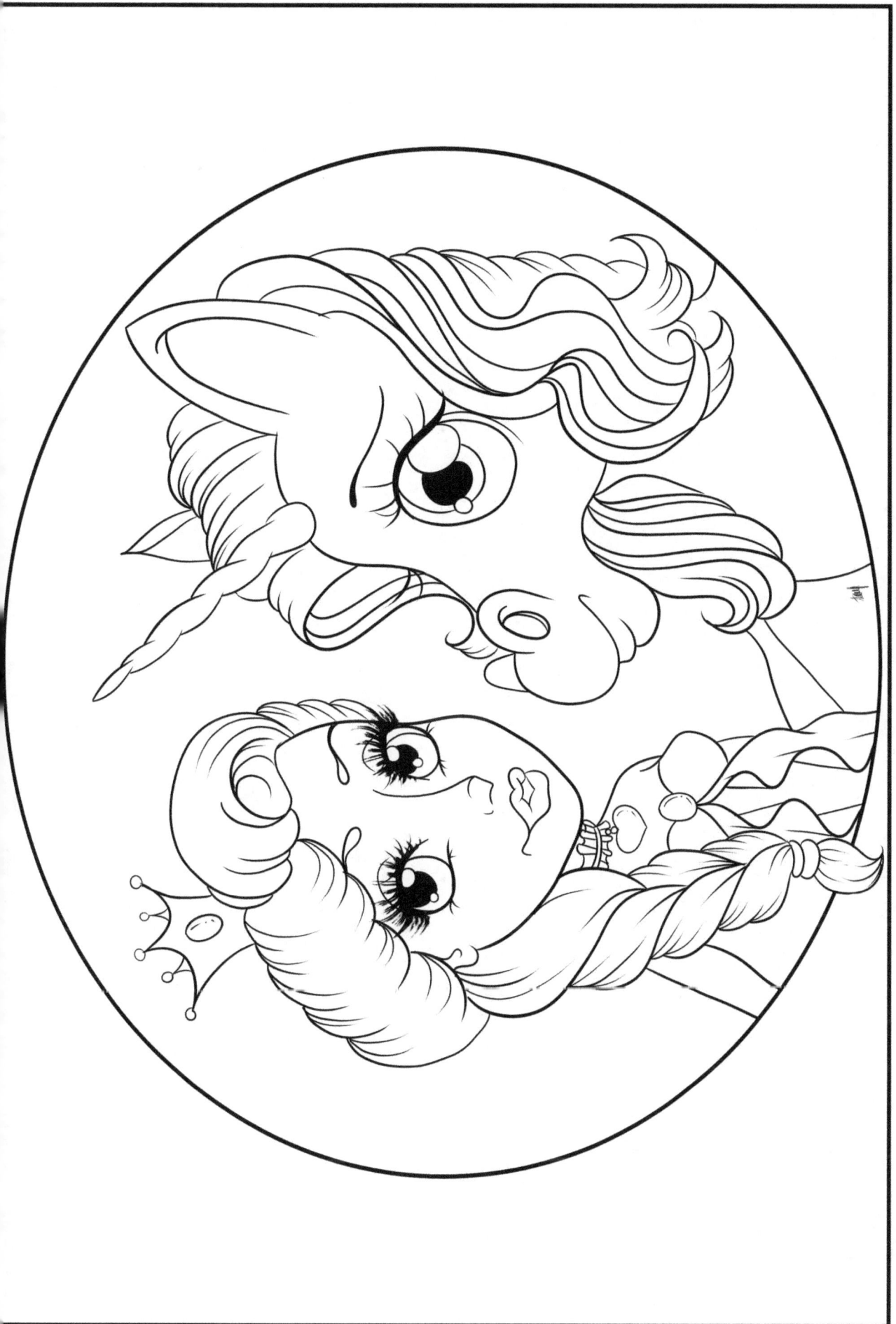

Illustrations by T.
Tamara van Wijk